Amazing Animals of the OCEAN

written by Christina Wilsdon
reviewed by Robert E. Budliger

Silver Dolphin
San Diego, California

Silver Dolphin Books

An imprint of the Baker & Taylor Publishing Group
10350 Barnes Canyon Road, San Diego, CA 92121
www.silverdolphinbooks.com

ART AND PHOTOGRAPHY CREDITS

(t = top, b = bottom, l = left, r = right, c = center)

Contents

What Lives in the Ocean?

Fish as big as buses, animals that look like flowers, eight-legged creatures that squirt ink—these are just a few of the amazing animals that live in the ocean.

The ocean is home to more than 200,000 kinds of animals, plants, and one-celled living things. Some scientists think a million or more new species will be discovered in the next few years.

Some ocean animals are big and well known—like sharks, whales, dolphins, tuna, and lobsters. But the ocean is also filled with living things that are so tiny, a dozen of them could sit on a dime with room to spare. Others are even smaller and can be seen only with a microscope.

Did You Know?

Scientists recently found about 20,000 kinds of microscopic living things in just 1 quart of ocean water—an amount of water that would only half fill a large soda bottle.

Floating Life

A layer of very tiny living things, called **plankton**, floats in the upper part of the ocean. The plantlike plankton use sunlight to make their food, just as plants on land do. The tiny animal plankton eat the plantlike ones.

What's That Word?

As you read, you will see words that are in **bold**. Look for them in the glossary on pages 36–37 to learn what they mean.

Sea and Shore

Where ocean and land meet is called the **coast**. The seas, bays, gulfs, and other parts of the ocean that poke into the land also have coasts. All these coasts add up to about 372,000 miles. That is enough coastline to wrap around the earth's middle at the equator nearly 15 times.

Coasts are filled with living things. Many sea creatures live on coastal shores. Some live in the zone that is washed by waves. Some live just beyond the water's reach. Other animals live offshore. Colorful coral reefs in warmer waters are home to many of these animals.

Some animals, however, live about as far from the coast as they possibly can. These animals live in the deepest parts of the ocean, where it is dark and cold. Some live on the ocean's floor and in the deepest places that humans have ever explored.

Did You Know?

The earth, moon, and sun all have gravity, a force that makes these objects pull on one another. The gravity of the sun and moon also tug on the earth's water. This changes the level of the ocean's water in most parts of the world four times a day. When the water level rises on a beach, it is called high **tide**. When the water drops away from shore, it is called low tide.

Stranded whales are a sad sight on a shoreline. Rescuers keep these pilot whales wet until they are returned to a safe place in the open sea.

Big Blue Marble

From outer space, the earth looks like a swirly big blue marble. The blue is the ocean, which covers almost three-quarters of the planet's surface. The land separates the world's ocean into five smaller ones: the Pacific, the Atlantic, the Indian, the Southern, and the Arctic.

Tide Pool Life

When it retreats from the beach at low tide, the ocean leaves behind puddles onshore. Puddles form in dips on mud flats or sandy shores. They form in basins among piles of rocks. These puddles are called **tide pools.** They can be as small as a cereal bowl or as big as a rowboat.

A tide pool is filled with life. Sea stars cling to rocks. Little crabs hide under the rocks. Bright green anemones spangle the pool like flowers. Tiny snails make wriggly trails in the sand.

Ocean animals live in a **habitat** where the temperature does not change quickly. Levels of oxygen and salt in the water change slowly, too. But they can all change in just a few hours in a tide pool. A small tide pool can heat up quickly in the sun. Its oxygen level then drops.

Animals in the tide pool live through these changes until the tide rolls in again. Anemones pull in their **tentacles.** Crabs burrow into damp seaweed. Many tide pool animals feed on plankton delivered by the ocean. Crabs eat seaweed and dead fish. Some tide pool animals eat each other.

A Salty Story

A tide pool's water **evaporates,** which means it turns into a gas and goes into the air. The tide pool starts drying up just like a puddle on a sidewalk. This makes the pool more salty, because there is less water to hold the same amount of salt.

Star Bright

A sea star eats other animals. It can open a clam by clasping it with its arms and steadily pulling on the shell. As soon as a gap opens, the sea star's stomach bulges out of its body. It covers the clam's body and digests it. Then the stomach slips back into the sea star's body.

A tide pool looks as if it would be a safe, cozy place to live in. But a tide pool also presents challenges for animals living in it—ones that ocean animals don't face.

Shore Leave

Some animals are most at home in the water, but they need to use the shore for parts of their lives.

Sea turtles live in the ocean, but they are all born on land. Female sea turtles drag themselves up on beaches to lay eggs in the sand. They head right back into the ocean when this job is done. The babies also dash toward the ocean as soon as they hatch.

The green sea turtle starts life as an egg that looks like a golf ball. The hatchling that pops out of the egg is about 2 inches long. The baby sea turtle drifts with the waves at first, feeding on tiny animals. It spends a few years at sea growing up. As an adult, it eats only plants and **algae.**

A female green sea turtle may spend 20 years in the ocean before coming back to the beach where she hatched. Then she will climb ashore there to lay her own eggs.

Fish Out of Water

Some fish come ashore from time to time. Fish called grunions wriggle ashore on parts of Southern California's coast during an extra-high tide. They lay their eggs in the sand. Then the surf sweeps the grunions back into the ocean. When another extra-high tide sweeps up the beach two weeks later, the eggs are ready to hatch.

Did You Know?

Seals also come ashore to give birth. Harp seals gather in large herds on icy shores in the early spring to have their pups. The seal pups stay on land, drinking their mothers' rich milk. Pups drink milk until they are about two weeks old. By the time a pup is about a month old, it has shed its baby fur. It starts to swim and eat fish in the water. On land, its main **predators** are polar bears and people. Now it must beware of sharks and killer whales, too.

Sea turtles like this loggerhead are in danger because so many people are building on their nesting places.

What Is a Coral Reef?

Colorful coral reefs are just offshore in warm tropical seas. A coral reef looks like a beautiful flower garden. But no plants grow there. The bright colors and strange shapes belong to animals. They share a habitat that has been built over many years by tiny, soft-bodied animals called **coral polyps.**

Coral polyps are related to jellyfish. A single coral polyp is like a small, squishy tube. It has a mouth but no brain. Stinging tentacles wave around the mouth. A polyp uses its tentacles to catch plankton to eat.

Coral polyps that build reefs live in large groups called colonies. Each polyp makes a hard tube and lives inside it. This tube is called its skeleton. The polyp also makes a kind of skin that goes over the outside of its skeleton. This skin joins up with the skins of the polyps around it.

Tiny plantlike living things called algae live inside many kinds of corals. They often give the coral its color. A coral reef grows over time because the polyps' skeletons remain in place after the polyps die. New polyps build on top of these old skeletons, and the reef grows larger. It may start to look like an underwater forest of strangely shaped trees.

Dirty Fish?

Fish live in water, so you'd think they are always clean. Not so! Fish suffer from pests called **parasites**. Parasites

may suck blood and weaken a fish. So little fish called cleaner wrasses keep other fish clean. They eat the parasites and also nibble off any flecks of dead skin. The wrasses get a meal, and the bigger fish gets a good scrubbing.

Reef Life

Stripes, spots, colors, dots—coral reef fish dazzle the eye. A reef may include as many as 150 kinds of coral! By day, the reef is a riot of color as fish swim about, searching for food. Their bright colors help them find mates, too.

At night, while many colorful fish lie low, other reef animals get busy. Squid and octopuses creep out of cracks in the reef. Sea urchins, sea stars, and crabs crawl about in search of food.

Animals called sponges don't need to leave home to look for food. A sponge simply filters plankton from water flowing through tiny holes in its surface. Tiny fuzzy cells inside its body help keep the water moving through it. Sea slugs, sea stars, and even turtles feed on sponges. Hermit crabs and shrimp sometimes live inside them.

Parrotfish feed directly on the corals' skeletons. A parrotfish's strong teeth can scrape algae off coral, but it comes with some stony skeleton. The parrotfish digests the algae, and any bits of skeleton pass out of its body in its droppings.

Room to Rent

A coral reef can be a crowded place. Finding a place to live isn't always easy. Some sponges, like these, solve this problem by making a poison that kills coral polyps. This sure helps them clear a place for themselves!

Ouch!

Lionfish have spines in their fins that are loaded with **venom**. The fish uses this venom to defend itself against predators. It doesn't need venom to catch fish to eat—it just snaps them up!

Hunters of the Reef

Many reef animals are predators. Cone snails sting fish, worms, and other snails. Other snails eat polyps, clams, sea stars, and sea urchins. Sea slugs eat sponges and anemones. Pistol shrimp snap their claws to shoot down fish with "shock waves"—sharp bursts of pressure like underwater cracks of thunder.

The biggest predators of the reef are sharks. Whitetip, blacktip, and gray reef sharks are familiar sights in many Pacific Ocean coral reefs and some Indian Ocean reefs. Whitetip sharks often spend the day lolling in underwater caves in groups. At night, they come out to eat octopuses, crabs, lobsters, shrimp, and fish. Blacktip reef sharks also eat fish, octopuses, lobsters, and shrimp.

Blind sharks live on coral reefs along parts of Australia's coast. There they feed on anemones, shrimp, crabs, and cuttlefish. A blind shark can see just fine. Its name comes from its habit of shutting its eyes when it is lifted out of the water.

In Plain Sight

Wobbegongs are wide, flat sharks that live near Australia. They are covered with spots and splotches, which help them blend in with coral. When fish come close...*chomp!*

Beware!

Moray eels hide in cracks and holes in a reef. When a fish swims by, a moray lunges out to grab it with sharp teeth. Moray eels can even eat big meals such as squid and large fish. A moray has a second set of jaws in its throat that helps it swallow its super-sized servings.

Gray reef sharks tend to swim along the outside of coral reefs near the seafloor. They swim long distances as they hunt for food.

Seeing Seabirds

Gulls, puffins, terns, and other seabirds spend much of their lives flying over the ocean and feeding from it. Some visit land only to lay eggs and raise their young.

Many seabirds have huge wings that help them soar for long stretches of time. The biggest wingspan belongs to the wandering albatross. This bird's wings measure up to 12 feet from tip to tip.

An albatross rarely needs to flap its wings because wind blows almost nonstop across the Southern Ocean. If the wind dies, the albatross floats in the water until the wind starts to blow again. An albatross can fly thousands of miles a year as it searches for squid and fish to eat.

Did You Know?

Sooty shearwaters hold the record for the longest **migration**. They fly from New Zealand, where they nest, to feeding areas in the North Pacific, then back to New Zealand. That is almost 40,000 miles in one year—a distance that is nearly twice around the earth!

Some birds dive headfirst into the water from high in the air to catch fish. They fold their wings, point their bills toward the ocean, and enter the water like darts. This is called plunge-diving. Gannets and brown pelicans hunt this way. Other seabirds, like storm petrels, flap just above the ocean's surface, dabbing their feet in the water as they snatch up tiny animals.

An albatross takes one mate for its entire life, which can be from 50 to 80 years long.

Birds That Can't Fly

Penguins are seabirds that can't fly in the air but fly fast and deep in the water, flapping furiously as they chase fish. The biggest penguin is the emperor penguin, which lives in Antarctica.

Lots of Arms

Octopuses and squid are eight-armed animals found only in saltwater. Their arms are lined with rows of suction cups called suckers. These animals can wriggle their way along the seabed with their arms, as well as cling to rocks with their suckers.

Squid also have two tentacles that are usually longer than their arms. They use the tentacles to catch fish and shrimp.

Suckers and long arms come in handy for grabbing **prey**, too. An octopus drags its prey to its mouth, which is at the base of its arms. It has a beak as sharp and strong as a parrot's for biting its prey.

Octopuses and squid have several ways to protect themselves. One way is to speed away from a predator by taking water into its body, then pushing it out through a funnel-shaped part called a siphon. This action is called **jetting**.

Most octopuses and many squid can change the color, pattern, and texture of their skin in the blink of an eye! They change color to blend in with their background so they won't be noticed by predators.

Did You Know?

If an octopus loses one of its arms, it can grow a new one.

Inked Out

This cuttlefish, a relative of squids and octopuses, can flee from a predator by shooting out a cloud of dark ink into the water. The ink hides it and startles the predator, giving the cuttlefish a head start on its getaway.

Something's Fishy

What does a fish have inside it that an octopus doesn't? A skeleton. Fish have a backbone and other bones just as you do. All fish have this in common, even if they are shaped quite differently. A tuna looks nothing like a sea horse, but they are both fish.

Fish breathe underwater using a pair of organs called **gills**. The gills get oxygen from the water as it flows through them.

Almost all fish have fins on their bodies. The tail fins point up and down. Most fish swim by waving their bodies from side to side so that their tails wag and their fins push against the water.

Some fish, such as the tuna, have very stiff, pointed tail fins for going extra-fast. A tuna doesn't wave its body from side to side as it swims—its power is in its tail.

Did You Know?

A flounder starts life as a fish with an eye on each side of its head. But as it grows, one eye slowly moves over next to the other eye. The fish also starts living sideways. Being a flatfish lets a flounder lie flat on the seabed, where it blends in with sand and stones.

Coral Reef Fish

Some of the ocean's most colorful fish live in places called coral reefs.

Longhorn cowfish

The longhorn cowfish's yellow body is boxy and hard. Only big fish with strong jaws can eat it. The harlequin tuskfish has blue teeth!

Harlequin tuskfish

The boldly colored clown fish avoids predators by tucking itself among the stinging tentacles of flowerlike animals called anemones. The clown fish's skin oozes a slime that protects it from the stings, but other fish must keep away. It's no surprise, then, that the clown fish is also known as the anemonefish.

23

Super Sharks

Like many people, you probably picture a shark as a fierce animal with huge, toothy jaws. But sharks come in many shapes and sizes—and some of them aren't a bit fierce.

The world's biggest fish is a shark that is so gentle that divers can stroke its back. It is the whale shark. A whale shark can be up to 40 feet long—a little longer than a big school bus. It swims slowly, filtering plankton and small fish from the water. Basking sharks and megamouth sharks feed this way, too.

Most sharks are torpedo-shaped and are swift swimmers. Some have different shapes. The angel shark has a wide, flat body with large, winglike side fins.

A hammerhead shark has a head shaped like a hammer, with its eyes at either end. Its wide head helps it find food. Some hammerheads even use their heads to dig up food or hold down struggling prey.

Did You Know?

Sharks do not have bony skeletons as other fish do. Their skeletons are made of **cartilage,** the same flexible material found in your ears and the tip of your nose.

The Great White

The most famous shark is the great white. It is one of the biggest sharks. It can grow to be about 23 feet long. Great whites eat fish, sea turtles, seals, and dead animals, as well as other sharks. This kind of shark is feared because it is known to attack people.

The usually harmless blacktip reef shark is named for the dark tips on all its fins.

A Sharp Cookie!

The little cookie-cutter shark has big, sharp teeth. It feeds by "kissing" the side of a bigger animal, then sticking to it with its suction-cup lips. Next, it chews a rounded bite out of it. Squid, dolphins, and even whales have scars that show they've been chomped by cookie-cutters.

Rays and Skates

Rays and skates are strange, flat fish with fins like bat wings. They are the sharks' closest relatives. Like sharks, they have skeletons made of cartilage. But instead of being shaped like submarines, most rays and skates look more like flying carpets flapping through the ocean. Scientists call the wide, flat side fins "wings."

Most rays and skates feed on the seafloor. They skim above the sand and mud like metal detectors on the prowl, eating snails, clams, shrimp, and fish without shells.

The biggest ray is the giant manta ray. Its wings measure about 20 feet from tip to tip. It can weigh more than 3,500 pounds—almost as much as three milk cows. This huge ray eats plankton that it filters from the water. It waves plankton toward its mouth with the two fins that stick out from its head like horns.

Zap!

An electric ray makes electricity in organs that are located behind its eyes, near the base of its side fins. It uses the electricity to stun fish, which it eats. The biggest electric ray is the Atlantic torpedo ray. It can be as long as a tall adult human and produce shocks strong enough to stun a diver.

Did You Know?

Rays and skates are members of a group that scientists call batoids. Batoids have fins that look like the wings of bats. Sawfish and guitarfish also belong to this special group of sea creatures.

The eagle ray slowly flaps its large, triangle-shaped wings up and down to push itself through the water.

27

What Is a Whale?

A whale looks a lot like a fish, but it isn't a fish. A whale is a **mammal**—a **warm-blooded** animal that has hair. A female mammal makes milk for her young. A whale does not have gills for breathing. It has a **blowhole** on top of its head and must come to the surface to breathe air. A thick layer of fat under the skin, called **blubber**, keeps the whale warm in the ocean.

Scientists divide whales into two groups—toothed whales and **baleen** whales. A toothed whale has teeth. Sperm whales, narwhals, and belugas are toothed whales. A baleen whale has no teeth. Instead, it has long strips of tough material hanging from its upper jaw inside its mouth. This material is called baleen. A baleen whale strains mouthfuls of water through its baleen to filter out food.

The biggest whale, the blue whale, feeds on tiny plankton animals called **krill** that look like tiny shrimp. A blue whale may eat up to 16,000 pounds of krill in just one day. On this meal plan, the whale can grow to weigh 200,000 pounds!

The White Whale

The cold Arctic Ocean is home to white whales called belugas. Belugas are gray when they are born and turn white as they grow. Unlike other whales, they can easily turn their heads on their flexible necks.

Both the gray whale (far left) and the sei whale (center) are baleen whales that feed on plankton. The black-and-white killer whale, or orca (near left), is a toothed whale that eats much bigger food, such as seals, sharks, and sea lions.

Finned, Not Fishy

Dolphins and porpoises are toothed whales. Sometimes they can be seen leaping in and out of the water, as if stitching their way through the waves. This motion is called **porpoising.**

By porpoising, a dolphin or porpoise can swim faster, because it is easier to move forward through air than through water. Each leap also lets the animal take a breath before diving back underwater.

Seals, sea lions, and walruses are ocean mammals that also spend time on land. A seal is graceful at sea, zooming through the water to catch fish. On land, it shuffles along on its belly, dragging its hind flippers. A sea lion has an easier time walking onshore than most seals do because it can rotate its hind flippers forward, then waddle on all four flippers.

Killer Whales

The biggest dolphins, the orcas, eat sharks, turtles, dolphins, porpoises, and other whales. This menu gives orcas their other name—killer whales. Orcas can grow to be as long as a big school bus. They are the fastest swimmers among sea mammals. An orca can zip along at a speed of 40 miles an hour.

Walruses

A walrus uses its big tusks like ski poles to pull itself onto the shore or a floating piece of ice.

Dolphins like these Pacific white-sided dolphins jump high into the air and then belly flop onto the water's surface. This is called **breaching***.*

What's in the Deep?

Far from shore, out past the coral reefs, are the ocean's wide-open spaces. Different kinds of animals live at different levels in this vast area.

Some of the animals live in a **twilight zone**. They light up the gloom by glowing. Ax-shaped hatchetfish have rows of lights on their bellies. Bristlemouths and little lanternfish are speckled with miniature lights on their stomachs and sides. These lights help the fish blend in with the little bit of sunlight that glows faintly in the water above them. It hides them from hungry fish below.

Glowing also helps fish lure prey. The dragonfish has a glowing whisker on its chin that attracts other fish, putting them in easy reach of its toothy jaws. Having lights also helps fish find mates. The pattern of lights helps them identify other fish of the same species.

Giant squid, sperm whales, and frill sharks also dwell in the twilight zone. A giant squid can grow to be about 60 feet long!

Did You Know?

Some fish and other animals make light when oxygen mixes with chemicals stored in parts of their bodies. Fireflies produce their own light this way. Other animals, including some fish, glow because their bodies hold pockets of small living things that actually produce the light.

Glowers

Dragonfish

Lanternfish

Hatchetfish

A sperm whale feasts on squid and octopuses. A sperm whale can dive as deep as two miles, and it can stay underwater for more than an hour! That gives it plenty of time for a long struggle.

Mysteries of the Deep

The ocean's dark zone is far beyond the reach of sunlight. Animals living there dwell in cold and total darkness. Without light, no plants can grow. As a result, there isn't a lot to eat in the dark zone.

Many deep-sea animals depend on bits of dead plants, animals, and one-celled living things trickling down from above. Sometimes, a feast arrives in the form of a whole dead whale!

Gulper eels have gigantic mouths. They lure prey closer with a flashing light on the tip of their long tail. Then they take in their prey with huge jaws. The eel's body can stretch to fit a fish as big as it is. An anglerfish, however, can eat fish twice its size.

Viperfish often move up into the twilight zone to feed at night. Most viperfish have lights along their bodies. Their teeth are long and sharp. A viperfish's stomach is coated with a dark lining so that any glow-in-the-dark meals it eats won't make the predator shine, too!

Deep, Secret Places

Deep in the ocean are places where hot water pours from cracks in the ocean floor. **Bacteria** living here can turn minerals in the water into food. Other animals such as crabs, shrimp, and snails live here, too. Some of them eat the bacteria. Giant tube worms have bacteria living inside them that help keep them fed.

How Deep?

The deepest place on earth may be the Marianas Trench. This trench is nearly 7 miles beneath the ocean's surface. Scientists explored it in a deep-sea **submersible.** Even at that depth, they saw anemones and other living things.

Deep-Sea Swimmers

Viperfish

Crossed-toothed perch

Gulper eel

Gulper shark

Glossary

algae: Plantlike living things that use sun, air, and water to make food

bacteria: A one-celled living organism

baleen: Strips of tough material hanging from a whale's upper jaw that filter food from water

blowhole: A hole at the top of a dolphin's or whale's head that lets the animal breathe air in and out

blubber: The layer of fat just under the skin of whales, seals, and manatees

breaching: When a dolphin or whale jumps out of the water and lands on its back or side

cartilage: The rubbery, flexible material that forms the skeleton of sharks, rays, and skates

coast: A place where the ocean meets land

coral polyp: A soft-bodied animal with a tube-shaped skeleton

evaporate: To turn from a liquid into a gas

gills: Body parts on fish that absorb oxygen from water

habitat: The environment in which a plant or animal lives

jetting: Shooting out water to move quickly away from danger

krill: Tiny shrimplike ocean animals in plankton

mammal: A warm-blooded animal that has hair (at some stage of its life) and feeds its young milk produced by the mother

migration: The regular trip from one place to another from season to season

parasite: A plant or animal that lives or feeds off another plant or animal, called a host; the host usually won't die, but will become very sick or weak

plankton: Tiny living things that float mainly in the ocean's upper layers

porpoising: A way some dolphins swim by leaping out of the water in low curves, allowing them to take a quick breath of air while swimming

predator: An animal that eats other animals

prey: Animals that are eaten by other animals

submersible: A strong metal craft used to explore the depths of the ocean

tentacles: Long flexible organs around an animal's mouth or head that help it move, grasp, and feel

tide pool: A puddle left behind on a shore when the tide goes out

tides: The regular rise and fall of the ocean along coasts

twilight zone: The layer of the ocean that is between 650 and 3,300 feet deep, and where very little sunlight reaches

venom: The poisonous fluid that some animals make in their bodies and inject into other animals by stinging or biting

warm-blooded: Having a body temperature that stays the same when the temperature of the habitat changes

3-D Model Instructions

Complete one puzzle at a time. Press out the pieces and arrange them as shown. Using the numbers on the pictures here, match the slots and assemble your 3-D ocean animals.

Sailfish

Sailfish are the fastest fish in the ocean, reaching a top speed of 68 miles per hour.

1. Line up the slots.

2. Push fin piece through all three slot

Orca

Orcas are often called killer whales because they eat sharks, turtles, dolphins, porpoises, and other whales.

Great White Shark

The great white shark is one of the biggest sharks and can grow to be up to 23 feet long.

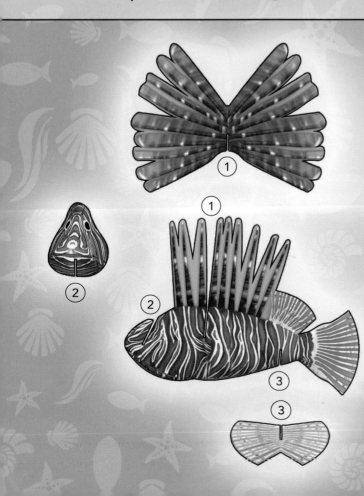

Lionfish

Lionfish have spines in their fins that are loaded with venom.

Diorama Instructions

Bring your own ocean world to life by building a beautiful diorama. It's easy!

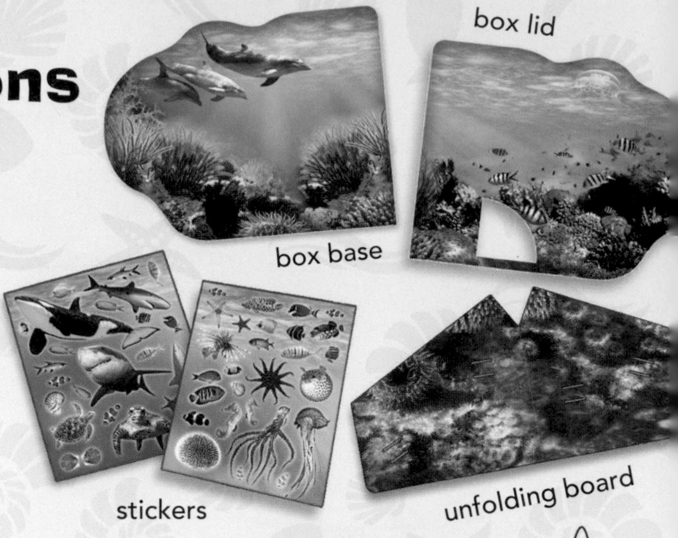

box lid

box base

1. The inside of the box lid and base will be the walls of your diorama. The unfolding board will be the floor. Decorate these with reusable stickers as desired.

stickers

unfolding board

2. Press out the floor figures, and fold as shown. Decorate with some stickers if desired. Fold, then slide the rectangular tabs through the floor slots, folding them underneath so the figures stand upright. The tabs and slots are all the same size, so you can change the position of the figures.

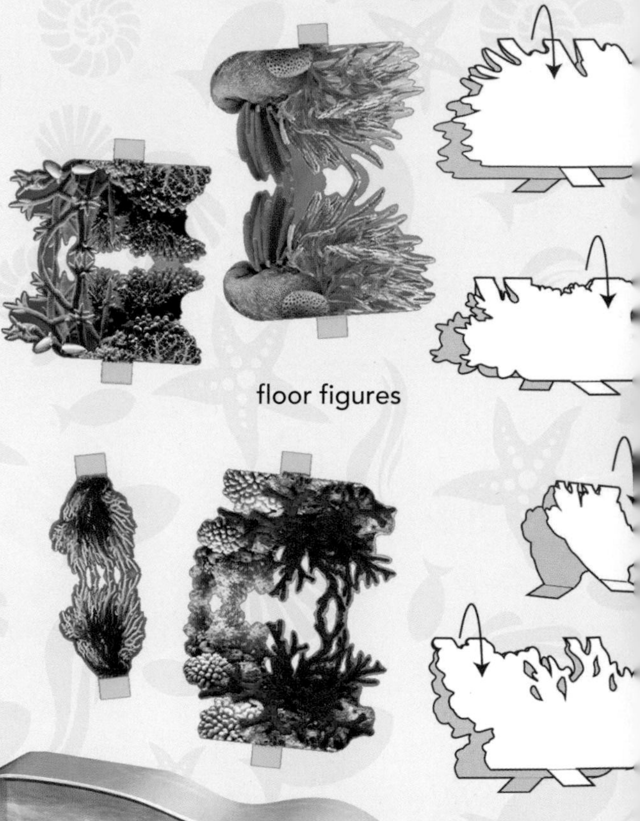

floor figures

3. Stand the box lid and base upright and at an angle as shown. Lay the angled back edges of the floor piece on top of the box sides. You're done!